SOMEBODY OUGHT TO DO SOMETHING

A Guide to Effective Action on Education Issues

"Never doubt that a small group of committed citizens can change the world, indeed it is the only thing that ever has"
Margaret Mead, Social Anthropologist.

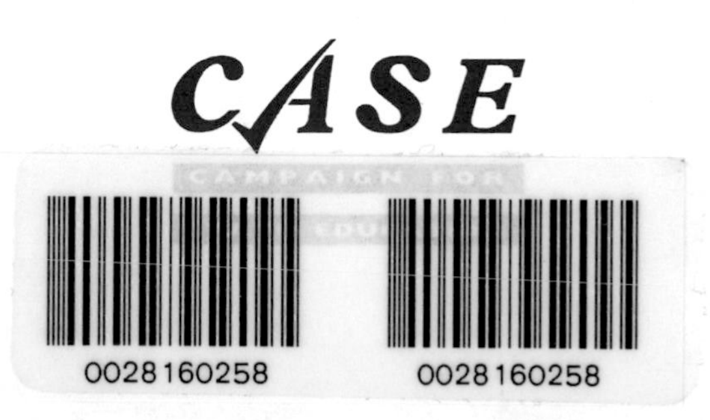

CASE — The Campaign for State Education — campaigns for the right of every child to the best state education.

CASE — is a membership campaign so needs **members** — if you are not already a member please turn to page 48, photocopy it, fill it in and send off your cheque and membership form **now**.

Even better — make several copies and get your friends to join.

STATE EDUCATION NEEDS A CAMPAIGN

Published by the Campaign for State Education (CASE) in association with Adamson Books
158 Durham Road
London SW20 0DG Tel/Fax 081 - 944 8206

ISBN 0 948543 50 7

Typeset and printed in Great Britain by
Business Stationery
150 Westway
London SW20 9LS Telephone 081 - 542 0505

This booklet was compiled by CASE members. CASE welcomes suggestions for inclusion in further editions. Please send them to Margaret Tulloch at CASE (address above).

CONTENTS

Planning a Campaign

Why Campaign?

Sometimes grumbling is not enough. Many people care deeply about educational issues - recognising the fundamental effect education has on the quality of all our lives and our children's hopes for the future. Such concerns can turn the mildest of people into effective campaigners. Campaigns do succeed - not always - but often enough to make it worthwhile. You will have moved the argument on, perhaps to be picked up later. At the very least you will have 'done something'!

Before You Start

Campaigns involve time, energy and commitment and tend to take over your life, for a while at least. Decide if you and your family can take the strain!

Whether a campaign is born of fury, frustration or simple disbelief at what is happening, its chance of success will be improved by an organised structure and clear, strategic thinking.

What do you want to achieve?

A campaign must have a point. Are there long and short term objectives? It is best to emphasize the positive - campaigning *for* something has more appeal than a negative approach. It is better for instance to 'Save Newtown High' rather than 'Say No to Closure'. Try to find good practice happening elsewhere which you can highlight. Call for this good practice to be established in your area.

Your initial impact is important. Don't cloud the issue with 'ifs' and 'buts'. Establish a name and a slogan. Be clear about the one or two main points you want to make.

What kind of campaign are you starting?

It's likely that your campaign will fall roughly into one of the following categories:

National issues

These may be:

- Long term campaigns which may involve changes in legislation or decision making by MPs or Ministers. CASE has national campaigns, such as the class size campaign, which members and local groups support. The local dimension is essential in national campaigns because it is local MPs who can raise an issue in Parliament. They do that most effectively when they have had information supplied to them locally or when they have to respond to local constituents. The media too are interested in specific examples of concerns which CASE is campaigning about nationally.
- Short term campaigns on national issues when government is about to introduce new legislation. Local campaigns are needed in every area to focus attention on a Bill in Parliament in the hope of getting it thrown out - or more realistically - changed - as it proceeds through its stages in Parliament. Your local MP is the major focus for your attention.

Local issues

These may also be long or short term. The decision makers whom you want to influence will be local and therefore easier to approach. There may be a need for long term campaigns involving the need for money for things such as nursery provision or school building programmes. There will be an overlap here between the responsibilities of local and central government.

There will also be much more immediate issues. A school is threatened with closure or a change of age range. A school is intending to opt out and introduce some kind of selection. Here there will be a clear deadline for a decision and a speedy reaction is required. This is the most intensive form of campaigning but may have a clearly successful outcome.

How can you get what you want?

- Who are the targets whom you want to influence? Are they local, national or both? Who are your likely allies?
- How can you achieve your aims? What are the best tactics to use?

As soon as you start to campaign about education one feature of the British education system will emerge. It seems to have been designed to enable buck passing of quite enormous proportions. Central government blames local government and vice versa. Now both can also blame governors and perhaps soon the Funding Agency! Getting representatives of all the decision makers in one place at the same time can sometimes move the debate along quickly.

Your campaign - step by step

1. Timing

It is best to pick a moment when your issue may be in the minds of potential supporters. For example, a campaign to introduce comprehensive education might be timed to start as the eleven plus results arrive.

2. Get together with others

It is very lonely campaigning by yourself and far more enjoyable to do it with others. It should be possible to find people who share your concern - even though you may be the first person to realise that a campaign is needed. Start by approaching people you know or try a letter to the local paper inviting others to contact you. You need a few supporters to sustain a campaign. If you don't get any interest, question whether it is an issue upon which to build a successful campaign.

If you are a CASE member, CASE can put you in touch with other members in your area and members in other areas who may be tackling a similar campaign. So join CASE now.

Set up an informal meeting to start the campaign off. Phone a few likely people and ask them to phone others. Include people who have contacts with other organisations in the area and so can publicise the campaign (see *People to Contact* p 16).

Small groups where the members can sustain each other can do far more than the sum of their individual efforts. After all you need someone to share the champagne when you succeed!

3. Organising the work

Spread the workload but make sure everyone is quite clear about what they have to do and when they have to do it. It is better to break up the jobs into manageable units and meet regularly to report back. Decide how often you need to meet and plan several meetings ahead so that dates are fixed in diaries.

You might find it worthwhile to do a skills audit, by asking everyone what particular skills they have and how much time they can offer. Remember many people will be unwilling to engage in public debate with politicians.

It would be useful to enlist the support of a lawyer to explain legal technicalities and an accountant to sort out the meaning of any financial information. People with experience of dealing with the press, graphic design (for the posters and campaign leaflets) and photography would also be a great help. However, if you have none of these you will find you learn very quickly.

4. Find out who makes the decisions

Talk to other local campaigners, to CASE, to local teacher unions, parents and governors groups. Start with the school by asking the headteacher. You need to know where the centre of power lies. It can be time wasting to target local councillors when the ultimate decision lies with the Secretary of State. However you will want to inform and influence them. Perhaps you should be encouraging them to support your campaign (see *Who Makes the Decisions*? p 18).

5. Make sure of any deadlines

Find out if there is a deadline for a decision to be made and work backwards from there. You may be able to pinpoint dates such as committee meetings when you will need to be active and attracting press attention. This is very important - success or failure may depend on it (see *Useful Information and Where to Find It* p 43).

6. Find some money

You will need money for photocopying, postage, printing and hiring halls. Use your contacts and supporters to find the cheapest way of doing this. Always ask for donations however small to support the campaign. Have two people standing by the door with buckets at the end of meetings. There may even be local benefactors who might make a donation to a good cause. You could organise a fund-raising event to give you a start. Keep all receipts for any money spent. Make sure you have someone keeping clear accounts and that it is someone's job to thank those who have given money or materials.

7. Research the issue

You must underpin your anger or concern with a secure base of factual information. Evidence will give your campaign credibility; it is needed to provide ammunition and to establish the extent of the problem you are campaigning about. It will also give you a means of assessing whether you are having some success. The sort of evidence you need will depend on your campaign. It may include, for instance, financial information, population trends and information about numbers of children leaving your area to go to schools elsewhere.

Build up a bank of information on the issue. Don't keep it to yourself. Reduce it down to a form everyone can understand and make sure that all supporters have the facts at their fingertips. This will give everyone greater confidence (see *Useful Information and Where to Find It p 43* and *Money Matters* p 36).

You may be dealing with people practised in argument and bland assurances. You will also meet people whose job it will be to point out the weaknesses in your argument. This may not necessarily mean that they oppose what you want but as public servants it is their job to provide answers for the politicians you are lobbying. Get someone to play devil's advocate and list every awkward question you may be asked and make sure you have the answers. If appropriate think of some alternatives or options to any proposals. This will mean your campaign will be seen as constructive rather than entirely obstructive. Remember many people including politicians should be given time to think about what you are saying. It is best not to force everyone into a corner - at least not at the start.

Being firm, fair and calm in public debate is most effective. The general public are more likely to be persuaded of the strength of your case. However make sure that everyone is left in no doubt of the strength of feeling which has initiated the campaign. You may have personal attacks and misinformation to cope with - try not to let them worry you. It is a sign that the campaign is having some effect.

8. Choose the right strategies for the task

There are several strategies you might use (see *Some Campaigning Strategies* p 11). You might focus on a specific day or event for a maximum effect. Prepare well and hit hard with several tactics at once: letters to the press, a press release, posters everywhere and the presentation of a petition all on the same day is well worth the effort it takes to co-ordinate.

The strategies you use will depend on your aim. A long sustained campaign will have to have highlights to keep everyone going and informed. A campaign to influence a decision to be taken at a particular meeting will have to build up to that day as a climax.

Try to be realistic about what you can achieve in terms of events so that you are not disappointed with a response which seems small but in fact is quite encouraging. If possible break up the campaign into manageable targets which you can achieve step by step.

9. Is it time to stop?

Try to review the campaign regularly. Look at your objectives and check how far they have been realised. You may have won or lost your campaign and so it will be obvious that it has come to an end. You must at some time review what has been achieved, what else is possible and how much energy you have left. If you do decide to give up make it a positive end by getting together to draw a line under your campaign and decide what you have learnt and achieved.

10. Build on what you have achieved by joining CASE

CASE needs activists like you. If you are not a member turn to page 48 now, photocopy it, fill it in and send it off. CASE membership keeps you in touch with others who share your belief in campaigning for the right of all children to the best education. CASE keeps you informed and your membership means that the national campaign is supported.

It may be that there are enough of you with the time to run a CASE group in your area - holding regular meetings, recruiting members, sending out a newsletter to members and campaigning locally and nationally. If so send for the leaflet - *Starting and Running a CASE Group* - and phone CASE for advice.

It may be there are not enough of you to share the amount of work needed for running a group but if one of you is willing to be a local CASE contact - speaking to the press if need be, recruiting members and being a two way contact for CASE, please let CASE know.

Some Campaigning Strategies

(See also *Anatomy of a Campaign* p 14; *Lobbying* p 24; *Dealing with the Media* p 27; *Running a Meeting and Speaking in Public* p 31);

- **Articles.** Your local newspaper may be interested in an article about the issue. Use your press contacts first (see *Dealing with the Media* p 27). Sympathetic organisations may be willing to put the article in their magazine or newsletter. National newspapers and the *Times Educational Supplement* are interested in local issues which illustrate a national situation.
- **Car stickers, badges and posters** are good campaigning tools, especially if they reinforce your name or slogan. Check Yellow Pages for badge makers etc.
- **Communicate** quickly with your supporters by a telephone tree. Have a list of phone numbers and phone ten people asking them to phone ten and so on until everyone is covered. You may need to make a quick response to events.
- **Demonstrations.** Some of the best protests are light-hearted without detracting from the seriousness of the purpose. Try and stage something which will attract the cameras eg coffins labelled state education or children playing instruments to defend a music centre closure. A badly attended demonstration may weaken your case so if you are going to do it be sure of a large and lively turnout. Be aware of the law relating to public gatherings. If you are planning an event contact the police more than seven days in advance. Be guided by them as to the conditions they wish to impose. Arrange for someone from the campaign to take photos, as well as the press - black and white prints or transparencies if colour is wanted. Then you can supply photos yourself with a press release if need be. Produce a simple leaflet so that everyone who stops to look at the event can take the message away with them.

- **Dripping taps** eventually build up into a flood. You can achieve quite a lot if you are rigorous and do nothing but refuse to go away.
- **Exhibitions.** If you can create a display which gets your message across simply you might use it on street corners or persuade schools and other organisations to display it for you.
- **Keep everyone informed** about how the campaign is going, including all your supporters and all local groups who might be interested. Use the telephone tree, local press and send a brief update to your supporters regularly. Keep a clippings file of any coverage you have or any other interesting developments. Keep CASE informed - we might be able to arrange more publicity and suggest ideas. Keep the opposition informed about your success too to show the strength of your campaign.
- **Keep everyone involved.** Make sure that all the campaign members can continue to put forward ideas. Have regular brainstorming sessions to decide new directions. Be prepared to admit mistakes and celebrate successes. Social gatherings keep up the spirits in a long campaign.
- **Leaflets.** These should be free of jargon and put the case clearly. Send a copy to the press. If you can afford to print a lot of leaflets you can stand in the shopping centre on Saturday morning handing them out. If money is tight it is best to try and target the people who might take up the campaign. They can be left on seats at school concerts etc; handed out to parents gathering outside primary schools best with the permission of the head or governors); governors meetings; car boot sales and on stalls at school fairs etc. Send them to PTAs and sympathetic organisations to distribute or better still to copy and distribute at their expense. LEAs might be willing for you to circulate publicity material via the schools courier - the regular circulation to all schools in the area from the LEA.
- **Letter writing.** MPs and councillors can be influenced by even a few letters on a single issue. Find out the correct name and title of everyone you need to write to. Encourage supporters to write short clear letters asking for a response. It is better that supporters write a letter in their own words than everyone sending the same letter. Since the advent of the word processor it is easy to send a standard reply to a standard letter. If people don t know what to say, set out a list of points they might make. Share the responses you have and follow them up. If you do get a standard reply there will probably be points which you made which the reply did not cover. Write again.
- **Meetings.** Use any meeting which people who might support your campaign attend - Annual Parents Meetings; PTA meetings; Governors Federations; Governor Training Meetings; School Fairs. Put leaflets on the chairs or hand them out. If you get an opportunity, speak briefly to draw attention to the campaign.

- **Noticeboards.** Community Centres, Health centres, supermarkets and libraries will have noticeboards which you might use. School noticeboards can be used with permission - even large trees in prominent positions. Supporters could ask shopkeepers to display a poster. Watch laws about flyposting. If you do put posters on lamp posts etc on the day of an event remember to take them away as soon as it is over.
- **Petitions.** Make sure it is correctly worded and includes the name and address of the petitioners. Make the wording simple so that people can understand quickly what they are being asked to sign. Have plenty copied so that supporters can collect a few signatures each. Make sure the deadline for return is clear. There is a correct format for petitions to Parliament which your MP should table. Ask for the leaflet about petitions from the Clerk of Public Petitions in the Journal Office of the House of Commons, London SW1A 0AA. If it is to be handed in locally arrange it so that you can get plenty of media coverage.
- **Publicity** is essential; its importance to a campaign cannot be over-estimated. Use every means at your disposal. Be prepared to repeat yourself many times. Remember although you may be living and breathing the issue most people won't know about it and may be very busy with other problems. First you have to inform them and then persuade them to do something about it (see *Dealing with the Media* p 27).
- **Public Meetings.** If well attended these can get a campaign off to a flying start by gathering a group of people who feel strongly about the issue (see *Running a Meeting and Speaking in Public* p 31).
- **Surveys.** These can prove very useful to prove a point and are newsworthy. You might be able to make comparisons between schools (best not to name them) or between your area and another. If you have contacts throughout the area you can use them to make sure there will be sufficient response to make the results valid. For instance a contact in every school might reply to a set of standard questions on problems over school cleaning. The questions will have to be devised carefully to ensure that the survey is not dismissed as invalid. Don't use ambiguous questions or give too many options. Don't ask too many open questions but give space for further comments. Try it out on a few people first to eliminate some of the potential pitfalls.

Anatomy of a Campaign

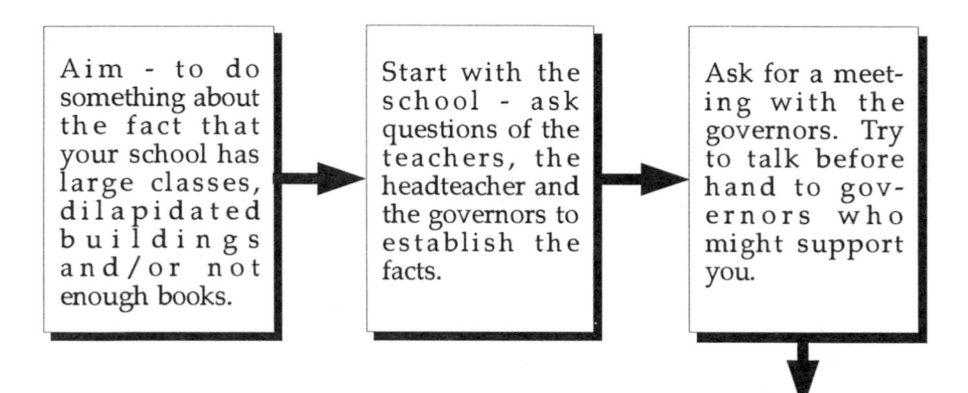

If the meetings do not help you achieve your aim then write to the Chief Education Officer of the LEA and the Chair of the Education Committee with copies to your local MP; unless the school is grant maintained, in which case go straight to your MP. If replies are not satisfactory ask for a meeting with the LEA and local councillors. This could be a meeting at the council offices with a few people or an open meeting at the school. Decide which best suits your purpose. Large meetings at the school will leave the LEA in no doubt about the strength of feeling.

Contact other schools in the area to see if they share the same problem. You could do this via any local federations there are, eg of governors, PTAs or teachers. Letters to local papers might also establish that this is a shared problem but it is best if this is a joint action from staff, parents and governors. If they have not been previously consulted, headteachers and staff are likely to be alienated by a letter in the press giving details of problems in the school. Use any other campaign strategies appropriate to discover the extent of the problem. You may wish then to go back to the LEA to arrange an LEA wide meeting.

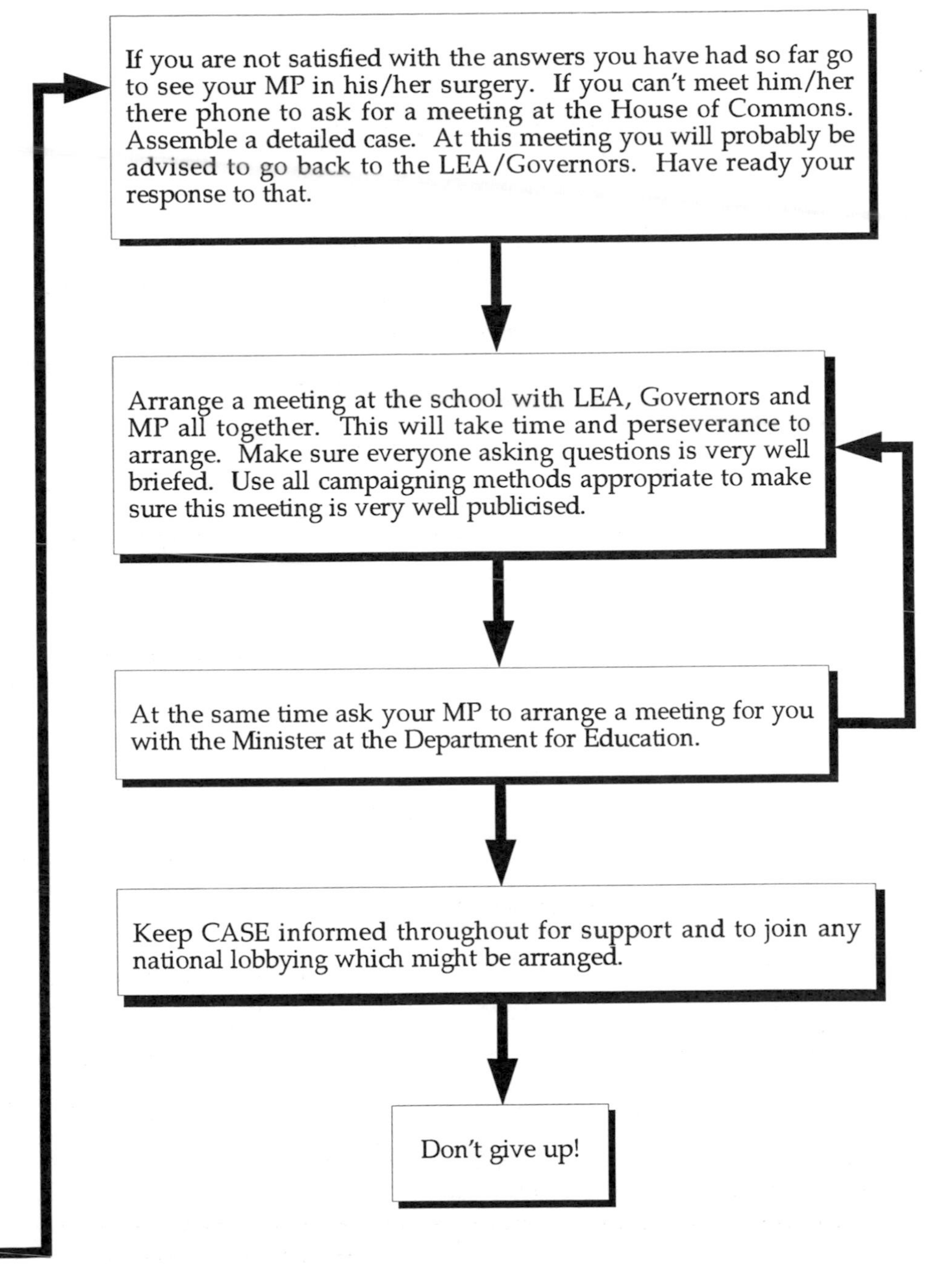
If you are not satisfied with the answers you have had so far go to see your MP in his/her surgery. If you can't meet him/her there phone to ask for a meeting at the House of Commons. Assemble a detailed case. At this meeting you will probably be advised to go back to the LEA/Governors. Have ready your response to that.
Arrange a meeting at the school with LEA, Governors and MP all together. This will take time and perseverance to arrange. Make sure everyone asking questions is very well briefed. Use all campaigning methods appropriate to make sure this meeting is very well publicised.
At the same time ask your MP to arrange a meeting for you with the Minister at the Department for Education.
Keep CASE informed throughout for support and to join any national lobbying which might be arranged.
Don't give up!

People to Contact

(For addresses of national organisations see *Useful Information and Where to Find It* p 43).

- Local schools, their addresses, telephone numbers and headteachers' names - from the LEA, your local library or the phone book.

- A list of school governors - your LEA or governor trainer may provide this or it will be in the Annual Report of each school. The name and address of the Chair of Governors will appear in the school prospectus.

- Secretary of local branch of National Association of Governors and Managers (NAGM) - contact NAGM to find out.

- Contacts for local branches of the teaching unions.

- PTA contacts in each school - you may have a local federation of PTAs - contact NCPTA to find out.

- Names and addresses of local councillors - with the ward they represent so that supporters can get in touch with their own councillors - from your local council offices or the library.

- Names and addresses of the Education Committee of your LEA and the Chair of the Education Committee - from local council offices.

- Local Diocesan Boards of Education responsible for Catholic and Church of England Schools - contact the national offices.

- Local voluntary groups, churches, community associations etc. There may be local branches of groups specialising in special needs or pre-school education.

- Local MPs and their agents - in the phone book under the party.

- Prospective parliamentary candidates and their agents - particularly vulnerable to pressure at election time - again from their party offices.

- Ministers in Department for Education - from the DFE.

- MPs on the Education Select Committee - from the information office at the House of Commons.

- Contact lists of the national and local media - in 'Editors' a booklet listing media names and addresses or from the local reference library.

- CASE

Who Makes the Decisions?

Finding out where the decisions are actually made - central or local government, governors or headteacher - can be difficult and there is only space here for a brief guide. Ask first at the school - then the local council offices and then the DFE to find out where the power lies.

Headteachers have overall responsibility for the day to day running of the school. They are the first people to approach with a concern.

Governors (particularly in grant maintained schools where they employ the staff and decide admissions criteria) have considerable responsibilities including the budget. Governors have the power to hire and dismiss the staff in nearly all schools. These responsibilities are shared with the headteacher who can choose whether or not to be a governor. In theory governors should set policy and headteachers implement the agreed policy. In practice most governing bodies are guided by the head on all decisions. Governors may choose to delegate some decisions to subcommittees. These subcommittees may have some non-governors as members. The governing body as a whole has the final decision on most issues at school level.

The school will provide you with a list of governors. You could ask to meet them. All governing bodies have parent and teacher governors who can be contacted. You can ask them to raise the issue at the next governors meeting. A letter to the Chair of Governors is another line of approach, a copy to the headteacher would be a good idea.

Local Education Authorities (LEAs) are responsible for the schools in their area, both county and voluntary unless they are grant maintained schools. Local authorities are elected every four years in local elections for local councillors. There may be one or more local councillors for the electoral ward in which you live. Not all local authorities are local education authorities - for instance many district councils do not have education responsibilities.

There are 116 LEAs in England and Wales. They have many responsibilities in schools such as providing the funds, reorganising schools (subject usually to the final approval of the Secretary of State), deciding admissions policy and the character of the education system - eg selective/comprehensive; two/three tier, employing the teachers and providing a range of support services. In voluntary schools governors have a greater role to play, in admissions to the school, raising funds for repairs and employing teachers.

The LEA's responsibilities are implemented through the work of an Education Committee, a subcommittee of the council. The Education Committee is made up of local councillors in the same political ratio as in the whole council. Some LEAs have parent, teacher, governor or church representatives on their committees.

LEAs employ officers to carry out the day to day functions of education. The Chief Education Officer or Director of Education will have a staff of officers with different responsibilities. You can contact them directly - make sure of the name of the person with whom you are in contact so that you can speak to the same person again - ask for a direct line number or extension.

If more and more schools become grant maintained LEAs will cease to have these functions. Their functions will be taken over by the Funding Agency when it is set up by the Secretary of State. (This is assuming the 1993 Education Act becomes law and sufficient schools in the area concerned opt out). The Funding Agency will be appointed by the Secretary of State and will be responsible to him/her. The Secretary of State is responsible to Parliament and therefore to you via your local MP. If a Funding Agency takes over total responsibility in your area for education planning then local councillors will have little influence and you must immediately go to see your MP with your concerns.

The Secretary of State for Education is responsible for overall education policy, including power over the curriculum and funding. He/she introduces legislation to Parliament. Many decisions are referred to him/her for approval from local education authorities. There are several Ministers or Parliamentary Under-Secretaries of State at the Department for Education each responsible for certain parts of education policy. They are answerable to Parliament and therefore you can reach them by contacting your local MP. MPs can arrange for their constituents to see a Minister.

You can also make a direct approach to the Department for Education. Phone first (see *Useful Information and Where to Find It* p 43) to check which branch of the DFE would be appropriate to contact. The Department for Education has numerous civil servants. Letters addressed to the Secretary of State from members of the public will usually receive a reply from a civil servant. You may be able to speak to the relevant branch of the department by phone. Again ask for names and direct line numbers so that you can speak personally to the civil servant next time. If you know what questions to ask, the civil servants will be very helpful. You have to be prepared to spend some time on the phone finding the right person.

Examples of campaign issues and where the decisions are made and can be changed

A Bill in Parliament

This would be introduced to Parliament by the Secretary of State for Education. The final decision is with Parliament: both the House of Commons and the Lords. The Bill can be amended as it goes through Parliament (see *From Bill to Act - The Parliamentary Procedure* p 34). Campaigning about a Bill would mean intensive lobbying of your local MP both by writing and going to surgeries. Check to see if your local MP is on the Standing Committee looking at the Bill. MPs would need to know the specific concerns you have about the Bill and its likely effects. Hold public meetings during the passage of the Bill to draw attention to it and invite local MPs so they can hear your views and explain their position.

Don't forget that Lords can also amend Bills. As Lords have less need to follow the party line they can often take a more independent view. In recent years the Lords have made commonsense changes to Bills. Lords often spend more time debating the Bill in detail. If you know any Lords contact them.

Cuts in the school budget

This may be as a result of cuts in the local authority budget (see *Money Matters A-Z* p 36). These would be decided by a full council meeting usually in early Spring, as the budget should be set by April 1st. You will need to keep your ear to the ground and then lobby councillors. Cuts may be because of government capping or a reduction in the SSA (see *Jargon Demystified A-Z* p 40) in which case you would need to lobby your MP and Government. It's best to call local meetings where the MP and Leader of Council are together to minimise buck passing.

It is possible that budget cuts in your school may be a problem specific to your school. It may be because of a change in transitional funding as Local Management of Schools becomes fully implemented (see *Money Matters A-Z* p 36) or because of a decision made by governors. Contact governors such as the parent governors and the Chair of Governors. The reasons for the cuts should be made clear to parents and staff.

School closure

This will be proposed by the local council (or possibly in the future by the Secretary of State or the Funding Agency under new powers). There may be plans to close or amalgamate just a couple of schools or there may be plans for a complete reorganisation of the education system. Particularly for the latter the council should consult with the whole community about its plans, presenting a detailed case. There should be a discussion document and public meetings. Although this consultation is not statutory (ie set down by law) if it did not take place protesters would have a good case to take the LEA to court for inadequate consultation.

Here there will need to be intensive lobbying of all local councillors. There will be two opportunities to do so as the plans will first be discussed by the Education Committee and then the full Council. If agreed the Council will then have to start a statutory consultation, issuing public notices about the plans in public places and local newspapers. There is a statutory consultation period of two months during which statutory objections can be made (see *Jargon Demystified A-Z* p 40). Such objections will mean that the proposals will have to go to the Secretary of State for approval/rejection. There is no time limit set on the time this decision might take.

School opting out

The opt out process can be set up by governors deciding to go to a ballot of parents or by 20% of the parents petitioning for a ballot. So at first, if you are a parent at the school, the governors making the decision should be approached to find out their reasons. A list of governors appears in the school annual report to parents or can be obtained from the school.

It is the ballot of parents which makes the decision to apply to the Secretary of State to opt out so parents will be lobbied by both supporters and opposition. There are rules governing the amount of campaigning which the LEA can undertake. A list of parents has to be made available to parents in the school so that any parent may contact fellow parents (quote section 60 of the Education Reform Act 1988) in order to lobby them before the decision.

If the parents vote in favour of opting out, formal proposals have to be made by the governing body and published in the same way as other changes. Statutory objections (see *Jargon Demystified A-Z* p 40) can be made to the Secretary of State.

Change from comprehensive to selective

Comprehensive schools admit all pupils regardless of ability; selective or grammar schools select pupils on ability. Such a change is likely to be a 'significant change of character' so statutory objections can be made (see *Jargon Demystified A-Z* p 40). An LEA may make this proposal for LEA schools. In this case lobby councillors then the MP as the Secretary of State has final say if there are statutory objections. In GM schools governors may apply to the Secretary of State to alter admission criteria in which case, first lobby governors, the MP and then make statutory objections.

Lack of nursery provision

Nursery provision is not statutory so local authorities do not have to provide it. It would be best to find out what other similar local authorities provide and lobby your local councillors. Contact Health Centres, childminding clubs, parents outside primary schools etc to reach potential supporters for a combined lobby. National pre-school organisations will give information and advice (see *Useful Information and Where to Find It* p 43).

Lack of provision for special needs

Here again provision varies from one local authority to another so it would be useful to find out what other LEAs provide. Local councillors will have to be lobbied. Within a school, governors have the ultimate responsibility to ensure that special needs are being met. Contact the Chair of Governors.

Parents with concerns about special needs often tend to be isolated within the education system. First it is essential that parents know their rights regarding special needs provision and statementing (see *Jargon Demystified A-Z* p 40). There are many organisations which can help (see *Useful Information and Where to Find It* p 43).

Parents need to get together with others to share problems and to lobby more effectively. To get parents together to share this problem call a public meeting by putting a note in the local paper eg ' Has your child special needs? Are they being met by his/her school?'. Contact one of the organisations which specialise in supporting parents with children with special needs (see *Useful Information and Where to Find It* p 43) and ask them to provide a speaker. Alternatively ask for a speaker from a local authority such as a senior educational psychologist. Make sure you collect a list of names and addresses of those who attend in order to contact them later.

Other concerns such as bullying and the need for provision for very able children could be tackled in the same way, as again parents often feel they are the only ones with this problem.

Other decisions eg planning applications affecting your school

Here local lobbying of councillors will be needed as it is initially a local decision. It is worth remembering that local councillors may speak on behalf of your school at committee meetings. Some local councils allow constituents or a representative of a groups of constituents to address committees personally. Find out the arrangements for this - you may have to give notice within a certain time.

Failure to get the school of your choice

Recent years have seen such exaggerated claims being made about parents being given more choice that parents might believe they have unfettered rights to select any school. In fact parents have only a right to express a preference. Whether that preference is met will depend on the size and type of the school, how near the parent lives and how many other parents have chosen it for their child. There are individual rights of appeal and the parent must be informed of them. The Advisory Centre for Education will give advice (see *Useful Information and Where to Find It* p 43).

If large numbers of parents have been disappointed this may call for a campaign - which again will be best started by getting aggrieved parents together at a meeting. It is essential to act speedily as there will be little time before the start of the new term. You will need to make sure who is responsible for admissions, the LEA or governing body of the school concerned. Start by asking the LEA.

Problems at school

The school should have a clear procedure for dealing with problems such as worries about individual teachers or school work. The class teacher, year leader or form tutor will probably be the person to speak to first, failing that the headteacher and eventually the governors. Contact the LEA for advice - there is a formal complaints procedure concerning a child's entitlement to the National Curriculum. Try to find out if other children are having similar problems and make a joint approach.

Lobbying

Lobbying is applying pressure to those people such as Ministers, MPs and local councillors who might, as a result of reasoned arguments and the numbers of people making them, be influenced to change their minds on a particular issue. The term derives from constituents arranging a meeting with their MP in the lobby of the House of Commons.

Be well briefed

It is very important to prepare your case well before meeting or writing to your local councillor, MP or Minister.

Research your case thoroughly. It may be that you need to ask your councillor or MP to find out some information for you. You might need to contact the Department for Education (address p 44).

Assemble facts which support your case. Do not make assertions which you can't prove.

Your letter should include:
- who you are
- why you are writing ie why current policy is wrong
- the changes you want to see and the action you want taken
- answer any arguments you think might be put by those opposing you

You might want to expand this brief onto several pages and send a covering letter. Send this information to the person you are going to see in advance of your visit so that when you meet, the time will be well spent by discussing the issue thoroughly. It might be that if you brief your councillor or MP in advance of the meeting he/she could write some letters on your behalf before you meet, so that you can have a more useful discussion.

Lobbying your councillor and how he/she can help you

The advantage of lobbying councillors is that they are local. They may send their children to local schools. You can see them more easily and more often than MPs. Find out from the Town or County Hall the name of the councillors in the ward where you live. Write or phone them to ask to see them. Many councillors have a regular surgery where their constituents can see them. Councillors will take up individual issues with the LEA officers and with the Chair of the Education Committee. If your local council has been guilty of maladministration you can take your case to the commission for Local Administration (Ombudsman) (see *Useful Information and Where to Find It* p 43). A local councillor can help you with this, or you can take your case directly to the Ombudsman.

Lobbying your MP and how he/she can help you

If you are not sure who your local MP is, phone your Town or County Hall or ask at the library. He or she will have local surgeries or you should be able to make an appointment to see him/her at the House of Commons. If you see him/her there, it is likely to be from Tuesday to Thursday. Many MPs are in the constituency on Fridays.

Phone either the local office or his/her secretary at the House of Commons. Alternatively if you are concerned about a particular school invite him/her to come there to meet a group of his/her constituents to discuss the problem. If you go to the House of Commons, tell the policeman at the door the name of the MP with whom you have an appointment. In the Central Lobby give your name to the attendants who will contact your MP.

Make sure the MP is well briefed by you about the problem. Discuss it thoroughly. Make sure he/she is aware of how the problem affects you and your children personally. MPs have to cover a lot of issues so it is a real help if they can have a clear picture about how, for instance a cut in a school budget might mean specific teaching being lost to the school. Be clear about what action you want him/her to take. If possible decide together on other further action he/she might take. Don't forget to thank him/her afterwards, including a reference to any further action agreed.

If he/she appears unsympathetic it may be because by asking what appear to be unsympathetic questions he/she can better build up a case to speak to someone on your behalf. Do not expect any MP to agree with you immediately. If you do not feel to be getting anywhere be persistent. Encourage other constituents to go and see the MP with the same problem.

It will help your campaign greatly if your local MP takes it up. The media will be more interested and the MP has local and parliamentary contacts. He/she might write to the Secretary of State on your behalf and will have a reply signed by a Minister rather than a civil servant. Ask for any copies of letters he/she might write and receive about your case. He/she may arrange a meeting for you with a Minister.

MPs can help focus attention on your campaign and get information which you might have had difficulty getting by asking a Parliamentary Question. A written answer will give detailed information. An oral answer will focus attention on the problem and will enable an MP to ask a supplementary question.

A Mass Lobby

Sometimes pressure groups organise a mass lobby of Parliament. Supporters are asked to contact their MP to meet a group of their constituents on a particular day at the House of Commons. The pressure group supplies briefing material for the use of Supporters. The organisers try to ensure that all MPs are contacted by one or more constituents. Publicity and negotiations with the Sergeant at Arms and the police will also have to be the responsibility of the organisers. Lapel stickers and publicity leaflets will give the message. On the day, events will be organised as well as the lobby. Large queues outside Parliament waiting to see the MPs usually attract media attention. If badly supported, mass lobbies may have a negative effect so they should only be organised if strong support is very likely.

Lobbying Ministers

Again sending a detailed brief before your meeting will be useful. Try to prepare your case very carefully - it is worth practising presenting your case to a friend who does not know the issue in detail. It is unlikely for you to have longer than 45 minutes. Your MP will probably accompany you and there will be civil servants present at the meeting. Don't forget to thank him/her in writing following the meeting - including a resumé of any action or comments agreed.

Dealing with the Media

There's no point in contacting the press, radio or TV to publicise your campaign if you haven't anything concrete to report. So a media campaign must be centred round a specific event, grievance or circumstance; eg a school losing teachers to save money; scrapping the school meals service; £3 million cut from the local education budget etc Identify the real problem, but try to give it a 'human' interest dimension (how it will affect individual children or parents) and then write a snappy press release. Journalists do like conflict - it makes for more interesting reading.

Warning. Be very careful that you don't expose a school you are trying to support to harmful publicity. Check that the head is agreeable to the school being named in publicity and, for instance, will welcome being contacted by the press or filmed for TV.

Media contact

You need to appoint one person as the media contact for your campaign. This person must be available during the day and has to be ready to act as spokesperson for your campaign - make sure he or she has a thick skin, doesn't mind being misquoted and has all the facts at his or her fingertips. Don't blame the spokesperson if misquoted, generally speaking all publicity is good publicity! An answerphone would be useful.

Try to be able to sum up the aim of the campaign in a few seconds - a 'soundbite'. Have answers ready to questions such as 'What do you want to achieve?' and 'What are you going to do now?'. It's a good idea to prepare a checklist of points to keep by the phone so the media contact doesn't always have to check back to someone else when asked questions by journalists.

Presentation

Most people, including journalists, are basically lazy - so do their job for them by a concise press release. Keep it to one page in double spaced type. Give the story a catchy headline.

There must be a contact name - preferably only one, but two at the most. Journalists like instant gratification - the issue has to be a very hot one for them to be bothered to ring someone else for the story.

You can do three press releases for a major event you are arranging; in advance to give journalists time to arrange to be there; just before it happens; afterwards for those who didn't come and might like to take it up.

What a press release should include
(see *example opposite*)

(1) Name and contact address for your campaign

(2) Date - including an embargo if you really want the information kept until a certain date. This is most useful if you are holding a meeting at which a speaker is likely to say something newsworthy and has given you a quote. You may want to coincide with a particular event such as the publication of a Bill. Otherwise it is best to have an immediate release.

(3) Heading - explaining the particular newsworthy event

(4) Content should include Who? What? When? Where? Why?. Include a quote from a named source if possible

(5) Contact - give day and evening numbers if possible

(6) Supplementary Information - background information which is more detailed and is not part of the press release

Do your homework
Find out the names of local/national newspaper journalists who write about education. Don't be afraid to phone up and ask the newsroom. Listen to all the local radio stations, and watch TV programmes - don't try to contact the presenters because they are only 'front men or women'. Make sure you keep an up-to-date list of names, direct phone lines and fax numbers. Journalists work increasingly by fax, so if you can use one it will be a great help. Faxing a press release has more impact and immediacy than sending it by post. Personal contacts with a reporter are very important to ensure continuity of reporting. You might give the press questions for them to ask the opposition so that the subject gets a thorough discussion. Ask the press for the dates of the deadlines they have to meet.

CAMPAIGN FOR STATE EDUCATION
158 Durham Road, London SW20 0DG **(1)**

PRESS RELEASE **(2)**
March 15th

START

NO MORE THIRTYSOMETHINGS SAY ANGRY PARENTS **(3)**

Thousands of parents, teachers and governors are supporting the CASE class size campaign.

CASE spokesperson Iva Hadenough said -

'The campaign is attracting wide support. All children deserve to be taught in small classes, not just the children whose parents buy private education'.

The campaign is calling for a legal maximum of thirty pupils per class. A public rally will be held on April 1st outside the House of Commons, Westminster. Class sizes are rising. CASE believes that large classes mean that children are not getting enough time with their teachers and that standards will improve if a legal maximum is introduced as in Scotland. **(4)**

END

CONTACT Iva Hadenough am 071 000 1111 pm 081 000 1111 **(5)**

CASE campaigns for the best education for all children. Membership is open to all who care about state education - including parents, teachers and governors. Class sizes in England and Welsh primary schools have been rising in recent years. Over a quarter of all primary children are now in classes over 30. **(6)**

Different types of exposure you may get

1. Television. This has the most impact - people remember when something has been on television and politicians are most wary of adverse TV exposure. So getting your campaign some TV coverage however small is a major breakthrough. However there has got to be a visual element in TV coverage - a demonstration at the school gates, a march etc. You will only get two or three minutes to make your point so make sure you can sum up your campaign in a couple of sentences. Anything longer is likely to be cut.

2. Radio. There is far more local radio now with the increase in the number of local FM stations. Listen out for access shows, local news programmes, phone-ins etc. Use the phone-ins to make your point. Make a spokesperson available for a live interview. It isn't nearly as nervewracking as TV. Remember not to speak too close to the microphone as every intake of breath is clearly heard! If you are asked to do a live interview ask the interviewer which question they will be asking first to give you a few minutes to organise your thoughts.

3. Newspapers - local and national. Local newspapers are always keen on local stories involving children - make sure you provide a photo opportunity and invite them to send a photographer to any event you are arranging. National newspapers need to have it made clear that your local issue has a national dimension - this is harder to do but if the issue is sufficiently controversial you could make an impact. The nationals, particularly the tabloids, like to expose 'troublemakers' so make sure you aren't doing or saying anything which might be used by any possible opponents to discredit you or your campaign. This is particularly important when children are involved.

Try to get a local paper to take up your campaign. Don't be too proud to let them think it's all their idea! Target local free sheets that may have column inches to fill and haven't the money to employ many reporters!

Don't underestimate the impact of letters to the editor. It's possible to get them into national papers - much easier in local ones. Letters to local papers about a local issue can help to alert the newspaper to your campaign - providing a two pronged attack. If an editor gets twenty letters on a particular issue he or she is likely to print one, so a couple of well written letters and many short ones making the same points will probably ensure that one is printed. When writing letters to papers make your points in separate paragraphs so that if they decide to cut five lines at least the rest is reasonably coherent.

4. Magazines. Most magazines work to a schedule which makes it difficult to get an immediate response - but you could work on a longer-term background story for them or write letters to the editor about your particular campaign.

Running a Meeting and Speaking in Public

Organising a Public Meeting

Decide the purpose of the meeting - is it to give information or to be a public debate? Fix on a few dates and contact the speakers to find a suitable date. Confirm in writing being clear what you are asking your speakers to talk about and for how long. Check if they want an overhead projector or other visual aid. If possible try to ensure by contacting others who have heard them speak that your suggested speakers will be reasonably lively and unlikely to alienate your audience.

Publicity is very important indeed - you will need posters in public places making sure you include time and place clearly. Small handbills which can be distributed via any network you have will be useful. If the venue is little known include a map showing bus routes etc, in the posters and handbills. Take out adverts in the local press. Use a telephone tree to get people there. Send out press notices.

Find a venue which is accessible. Make sure it can accommodate the numbers you expect. Clarify how much it will cost, for how long. Find out if a deposit is required and if it is returnable if you have to cancel. If it is a hall you have never used before make sure you have a look at it sometime before the meeting. Arrange for a public address system if necessary. Make sure that if there is a hall secretary he/she know enough about you to direct enquirers to the meeting.

Arrange for someone cool headed to chair the meeting particularly if feelings are running high. The person chairing the meeting should not offer too many opinions - leave that to the audience.

Have some leaflets to put on the seats so that people can take away information and ideas for further action.

Arrive in plenty of time in case you have to find the caretaker because he has forgotten to open up. Put up posters at regular intervals showing where to go - particularly if it is dark.

Make sure the PA system, overhead projector, video are working.

Arrange the seating so that discussion is easier.

If possible try to have a back up speaker from amongst your supporters in case your main speaker fails to arrive.

Make sure you allow time for questions from as many people as possible.

Encourage everyone present to join your campaign and to let you know if they have particular skills to offer. Make sure that they know that all help however small and low profile is urgently needed. Collect names and addresses by passing a clipboard round the audience.

Try to finish on time to avoid people drifting out.

Thank your speakers. A bottle of wine or bunch of flowers to those who don't charge expenses is usually well received.

Make sure you have people on the door with a bucket for donations as people leave.

People often come up to talk to the speaker at the end of the meeting. They may be people who would be active supporters so enlist their support then and there.

Afterwards send out press notices saying what happened. Write to thank your speakers. Have a postmortem with all the helpers to thank them and to see if there are lessons to be learned for next time.

Public Speaking

Planning beforehand

It is important to have a clear definition of the topic to be addressed. If you have been invited to speak make sure you know what it expected of you. In your plan make sure you are clear about -

- who you are speaking to
- how long you have to speak
- your attitude to the topic
- ideas you want to get across
- the outcomes or conclusions available which you might consider.

It is best to put at least the guide points of your speech on cards and run through them beforehand preferably with a sympathetic critic. If you need to read out the whole speech, read it through several times so you know it more or less by heart otherwise you will turn off the audience by reading your speech rather than addressing them. It is better not to read your speech if you can avoid it.

Technique

Seize the attention of your audience at once with a slight pause. Bear in mind audience attention span which is always less than you think. Don't speak too quickly and vary the pitch, tone and rhythm of your speech. Use the right vocabulary so that your audience does not feel excluded by your use of jargon. Don't distract attention with distracting body language such as rocking from side to side, fiddling with your glasses or waving your arms too much. Try to look relaxed, making eye contact with your audience some of the time and conveying conviction and self assurance. It is best to be brief - avoiding repetition. An overhead projector or flip chart with your main headings might be useful.

Questions

Make sure you allow for questions and comments. It can be more relaxing to answer questions than to make a speech and as much information can sometimes be put across. However questions can be hostile. Don't allow yourself to become too emotional or shout back if someone shouts at you! If you are asked a long question with several parts or several questions at once take notes before answering. Allowing the audience to comment as well as question may set up a debate within the audience which helps a great deal to make the issue clearer.

When it's all over

While it is still fresh in your mind make a note of what you have learned. Don't remember just a few hostile questions - they may be untypical. Ask someone who will give you a candid opinion of how you performed. Do not be downhearted by what you see as failure, you are certain to improve with practice. You may even enjoy it - at least it is an opportunity to get your views across without interruption.

From Bill to Act - The Parliamentary Procedure

Often legislation has been introduced after a process of consultation involving the publication of first a Green Paper, then a White Paper and then a Bill. All of these will be available from HMSO (see *Useful Information and Where to Find It* p 43). Lobbying your MP and Ministers at all stages of legislation is worthwhile (see *Lobbying* p 24).

Green Papers

A Green Paper will set out the government's intentions in broad terms and perhaps indicate alternative views on which government is seeking opinion. There have been no Green Papers in recent years in education. There is specific consultation about forthcoming circulars. Circulars set out guidelines (see *Jargon Demystified A-Z* p 40). Here the government will consult organisations such as CASE as well as statutory bodies such as local authorities. Individual responses can also be made.

White Papers

Even the expectation of a White Paper means that debate and discussion about the government's intentions will begin. The White Paper is a consultation document with a time limit for response. Recent experience does not indicate that great changes are made following consultation on a White Paper! During the discussion of the White Paper allies who might work to put forward amendments can get together. Once the consultation process is over, the Bill, based on the White Paper, is drawn up by the government's lawyers.

Bills

Most Bills start in the House of Commons and progress through there to the House of Lords. Except for certain Finance Bills it is possible for the process to work the other way. Whichever House the Bill starts in it must go through the same stages in the second House. If it is amended in the second House it must go back to the first one for consideration and approval of the amendments.

When a Bill is published the **First Reading** is the introduction of the Bill to the House. There is no debate. The **Second Reading** which follows in not less than ten days, allows the main purpose of the bill to be debated and a vote is taken.

Usually about two weeks later the Bill then passes to the **Committee Stage**. The **Standing Committee** discusses the Bill clause by clause and votes on any proposed amendments. The Standing Committee is made up of about eighteen MPs from all parties, roughly in proportion to the number of seats each party holds in the Commons. Standing Committees are always open to the public. Any committee member may propose amendments. The **Report Stage** to the whole House is usually about two weeks after the Committee Stage. It provides an opportunity for amendments to be tabled and those accepted by committee to be re-examined. **The Third Reading** often follows almost immediately.

The Bill then passes to the other House where it goes through the same procedure. The Committee Stage in the House of Lords takes place in the whole chamber. Unless amendments are agreed at this stage the Bill is then given **Royal Assent**. If it is amended then the Bill goes back to the House which introduced it for consideration of the amendments. If they are not accepted the Bill may have to go back for further discussion. The Commons will eventually have their way - in the end the House of Lords can only delay a Bill for a year. The government can then reintroduce it and the Lords have to pass it as it will have been passed twice by the Commons.

Education Select Committee

The Education Select Committee is not involved in the process of legislation leading to an Education Act. The Select Committee is an investigative committee, empowered to take evidence from Ministers, civil servants and others. The Committee can choose to look at particular areas of interest to them. They can carry out an effective scrutiny of the workings of government if they wish. The final report will contain their findings and recommendations. Ministers usually publish a report in response to the final report of the committee.

This Committee meets regularly, normally in public. It is made up entirely of backbenchers with a membership of about eleven, weighted slightly in favour of the governing party. Its membership lasts for the duration of a Parliament. The Chair can be from the opposition or the government. The proceedings of the Committee and its final report are published by HMSO as is the Ministerial response. These reports can provide useful evidence for campaigns. You can write to the Select Committee by writing to the Clerk whose name will be available from the House of Commons Information Office.

Money Matters A-Z

Aggregated Schools Budget (ASB)

This is the amount of the LEA General Schools Budget (see below) which is delegated to schools after money spent on excepted items is taken out. Excepted items can be mandatory such as capital expenditure or discretionary such as home to school transport. 80% of the ASB has to be delegated to schools on the basis of pupil numbers. The DFE considers that the proportion of the Potential Schools Budget delegated to schools (see below) is a better guide to the amount which an LEA is spending on central services.

Age Weighted Pupil Unit (AWPU)

This is the amount of money which each pupil carries. It will vary with the age of the pupil and the LMS (see below) scheme. The AWPU multiplied by the number of pupils of that age in the school shows how much money is provided in the school's budget in relation to the number of pupils.

Capitation

This is money spent on books and equipment in the school. It is often expressed per pupil.

Capital spending

This is money spent on particular projects - such as buildings rather than **recurrent** spending which is the regular expenditure to maintain the service. Every year the government publishes plans for capital spending on schools. Usually this involves giving permission to LEAs to borrow money to finance capital projects.

General Schools Budget (GSB)

This is the total planned expenditure by the LEA on all schools including the amount delegated to schools and all funding retained centrally.

Grants for Education Support and Training (GEST)
This is government money which LEAs are required to bid for. GEST funding is targetted so that LEAs may have to submit a bid for a particular project which is in line with current government thinking about what is required. Recent examples of GEST funding have been to pay for the implementation of Local Management of Schools. GEST funding does not form part of the Aggregated Schools Budget (see above).

Local Management of Schools (LMS)
This may be known as Local Financial Management. It is the system of school funding introduced by the Education Reform Act 1988, which devolved education spending into individual schools under a formula. The formula is based primarily on the number of pupils in the schools and other factors, including special needs. LMS schemes are set up by LEAs and have to be approved by the DFE. They may differ from one LEA to another. Circulars 7/88 and 7/91 set out government policy on LMS. Details of the LEA's scheme for Local Management of Schools (LMS) will be available from the LEA. Schools will also have a copy.

Because they have a delegated budget those managing the budget in the school can move money from one budget heading to another eg into capitation from the supply teacher budget - if there is any spare money. Schools are free to prioritise spending, within the overall constraint of the amount of money available overall.

Potential Schools Budget (PSB)
This is the amount of money which the LEA could delegate to schools ie it is the General Schools Budget (see above) minus capital expenditure; expenditure supported by central government grants; expenditure on school meals; home to school transport and transitional exceptions (see below). These items are considered by the DFE to be difficult to delegate or show huge differences across the country because of geographical differences. Comparisons would be difficult if these items were not excepted.

The DFE consider that the percentage of the PSB which is actually delegated to schools is a measure of how much education spending is being held at the centre rather than being delegated. The DFE produce a comparative list of local authorities based on the proportion of the Potential Schools Budget actually delegated to schools (see Public Spending by Local Government below). As of April 1993 (1995 for ex Inner London Education Authority authorities) LEAs are required to delegate 85% of PSB to schools. It is likely that this requirement will increase to 90% in 1995.

Public Spending

By Central Government. Plans to raise money in order to pay for the Government's public spending are set out in the Budget in March. The Government's expenditure plans are set out in the Chancellor's Autumn Statement following negotiations within departments and then between departments. These will have started at the beginning of the year. Ministers will put in bids to the Treasury in the Spring.

The Department for Education produces a Three Year Plan in the Spring following the Chancellor's Autumn Statement on public spending. It is available in reference libraries and from HMSO.

By Local Government. Local Government also sets its budget in March. This makes it difficult for schools which have only a few weeks to plan their budgets once the real amount of money which will be available becomes known.

Details of the local authority budget and the proportion spent on education will be available from the local authority and local libraries. Minutes of the Council and Committee Meetings will be in your local library. Also the working papers produced in advance of meetings may be in the library to enable you to find out what will be discussed.

LEAs produce budget statements under Section 42 of the Education Reform Act. These set out the amount allocated per school under several headings and the amount spent by the LEA on central services. Two sets of figures will be available - budget figures in April (ie proposed spending for the forthcoming year) and 'out-turn' figures in October (ie what was actually spent in the previous financial year). Section 42 statements should be available from the LEA and local libraries.

The Chartered Institute of Public Finance and Accountancy (CIPFA) produce sets of figures comparing education statistics and spending LEA by LEA in England and Wales. Some reference libraries have them. The Audit Commission plans to publish performance indicators which will also give useful comparative information (see *Useful Information and Where to Find It* p 43).

Revenue Support Grant

This is the grant annually given by central government to local government based on the SSA (see below) in order for the local authority to carry out its functions. Local authorities will also obtain revenue from the local community by means of the Council Tax, the amount depending on the level of capping which the government may fix. When provisional figures for SSAs and capping become available in late Autumn there are usually dire predictions of cuts in services, often fulfilled, although not always in full. This is where local campaigning has a part to play.

Standard Spending Assessment (SSA)

This is the amount of money which the Department of the Environment decides a local authority should be spending on its services, including education. It forms the basis of the government Revenue Support Grant to the local authority.

The Education Standard Spending Assessment is based on a calculation which involves the number of pupils and the Additional Educational Needs Index (AEN), free school meals, population sparsity and an area cost adjustment. The AEN is based on the proportion of single parent families, proportion of children of parents claiming Income Support and the proportion of children or parents born outside the UK, Ireland, USA or Old Commonwealth.

The Education SSA will be calculated under the headings primary, secondary, post-16, under fives and other, which includes youth service and adult education. LEA spending on education does not have to follow these budget headings. Post-16 provision is reduced in 1993 by the removal of post-16 college education from LEAs. Local authorities are not obliged to spend up to their SSA limit on education although most do and many spend more.

Transitional Funding

Funding available to schools and to some inner London LEAs to ease the transition to a fully delegated budget. For many schools this transitional period will come to an end in 1994. Funding for the transitional phase is not included in the PSB (see above).

Jargon Demystified A-Z

(See *Money Matters A- Z* p 36 for more jargon)

Assessment
A means of finding out what a pupil has achieved. 'Diagnostic assessment' is intended to show up the learning needs of the child. 'Norm referenced assessment' relates what the pupil has achieved in relation to the average achievement of others taking the test at the same time. 'Criterion referenced assessment' is geared to specific targets and is unrelated to what others have done in the same tests at the same time.

Standard Assessment Tasks (SATS) will eventually be carried out throughout a child's school life at KS1 (around age 7); KS2 (age 11); KS3 (age 14) and KS4 (age 16 incorporated in some way with the GCSE). The School Curriculum and Assessment Council (SEAC) sets out the procedures for the assessments at Key Stages. SEAC and the NCC are to be amalgamated into the School Curriculum and Assessment Authority.

CEO
Chief Education Officer/Director of Education. Head civil servant in a Local Education Authority. Not to be confused with the Chair of the Education Committee, a local councillor who will be voted in at each local election and then selected by his/her party to chair the Education Committee.

Circulars
These are government documents providing guidance and advice, often about the implementation of regulations (see below). They will be issued in draft for consultation. Circulars are not statutory (see below) and therefore can be changed without introducing legislation. They are available from the DFE publications section.

CCT
Compulsory Competitive Tendering. Local authority and some school services have now to be tendered for.

CTCs
City Technology Colleges set up by the 1988 Education Reform Act. A few 'independent' schools originally intended to be funded by industry with a technological bias. Running costs come directly from government. It seems that the government's intention is that voluntary technology colleges set up by promoters will further the concept.

Curriculum
What is taught in schools. The National Curriculum is laid down in orders issued by the National Curriculum Council with the final approval of the Secretary of State. It includes Maths, English, Science, Technology, Modern Languages, History, Geography, PE, Art and Music. Schools can teach other subjects in addition to the NC if time permits.

Judicial Review
A process by which the High Court uses its supervisory powers over the proceedings and decisions of lower courts, tribunals or bodies or persons who perform public duties (for instance LEAs, governing bodies and Ministers). A High Court judge has to allow for a judicial review to be carried out.

OFSTED
The Office for Standards in Education. This is headed by Her Majesty's Chief Inspector (HMCI). The members of OFSTED include Her Majesty's Inspectors (HMI). The responsibility of OFSTED is to establish a system of independent inspection of schools every four years and to advise the Secretary of State.

Maintained Schools
These are those maintained by state funding (independent schools are funded by fees paid by parents). Maintained schools include **county schools** which are funded entirely by the local education authority; **voluntary schools** which have a foundation, usually religious, providing the majority of the governors and some funding, with running costs provided by the local education authority and **grant maintained schools** where the funding comes from the local authority budget via the Department for Education or from the government via a Funding Agency. There are roughly 24,000 schools in England and Wales, of which about 4,000 are secondary. Primary schools take children up to eleven years old. Secondary schools have an age range from eleven to sixteen or eighteen. Some areas have first, middle and high schools; some other areas have infant and junior schools in the primary phase.

Mandatory / Statutory / Discretionary
In the case, for instance, of mandatory grants the LEA or relevant institution is obliged by law to provide them. Discretionary grants are only provided if the LEA decides to give them. Discretionary grants are disappearing as some LEAs make cuts. Statutory provision is that required by law or statute eg education provision for children on their 5th birthday. Nursery provision for under fives is not statutory so LEAs are not obliged by law to provide it.

Regulations and Statutory Instruments
Bills give the power to the Secretary of State to bring forward regulations or statutory instruments which give the detail about how the Bill will be implemented. Regulations have to be approved as a whole by Parliament. They are rarely changed when presented for approval to Parliament and, unlike circulars, have the force of law. Available from HMSO.

Significant Change of Character
These are changes to a school which require public consultation and therefore statutory objections can be made. Such changes would include for example a change in age range, a change from single sex to mixed or from selective (a school selecting pupils on ability) to comprehensive (admitting all pupils regardless of ability) or vice versa.

Standard Number
This is the number of pupils it is intended to admit to a school in any year and refers to a relevant age group. Standard numbers can be increased or decreased but the latter is more difficult and requires the permission of the Secretary of State. Open enrolment requires schools to admit pupils up to their standard number.

Statement
This provides details of the special educational needs of the child, following assessment by educational psychologists, doctors, Social Services etc. Schools should be provided with the support necessary to meet those needs, once the child has been statemented, over and above what the school gets in its delegated budget.

Statutory Objection
Proposals to make significant changes of character to a school can be objected to during the consultation period. Statutory objections can be made by ten or more local government electors, the governing body of the school concerned, any other governing body and the LEA. If statutory objections are made then the proposals have to be agreed by the Secretary of State.

Useful Information and Where to Find It

Addresses

Advisory Centre for Education (ACE) Unit 1B, Aberdeen Studios, 22-24 Highbury Grove, London N5 2EA Tel: 071 354 8321 A charity which runs a Mon-Fri (2 - 5pm) help line for parents and publishes several useful publications (see below).

Audit Commission 1 Vincent Square, London SW1P 2PN Tel: 071 828 1212 Fax: 071 976 6187 The Audit Commission monitors the effectiveness, economy and efficiency of public services. Publications are available from the HMSO.

British Dyslexia Association 98 London Road, Reading RG1 5AU Tel: 0734 668271 The national organisation for specific learning difficulties, has local groups.

CASE for addresses of local groups and other sources of information and help, other than those listed here (see p 2 for address).

Centre for the Study of Comprehensive Schools (CSCS) Queens Buildings, Leicester University, Barrack Road, Northampton, NN2 6AF Tel: 0604 24969 A network for comprehensive schools, operates a database of curriculum initiatives.

Chartered Institute of Public Finance and Accountancy (CIPFA) 3 Robert Street, London WC2 Tel: 071 895 8823 Publishes *Education Statistics* every year. Available in some reference libraries.

Children's Legal Centre 20 Compton Terrace, London N1 2UN Tel: 071 359 6251 Provides advice on children's rights.

Council for Educational Advance 2B Hillfield Road, London NW6 1QE Tel: 071 794 8657 Umbrella group of teaching unions and other educational organisations.

Department For Education (DFE)
Sanctuary Buildings, Great Smith Street, London SW1P 3BT Tel: 071 925 5000 Fax: 071 925 6000
DFE Publications, PO Box 2193, London E15 2EU Tel: 081 533 2000 Fax: 081 533 7700
DFE Statistics, Mowden Hall, Staindrop Road, Darlington, Co. Durham DL3 9BG Tel: 0325 392683

Education Otherwise 36 Kinross Road, Leamington Spa, Warwickshire CV32 7EF Tel: 0926 886828 Helps parents seeking to educate their children out of school.

Further Education Funding Council (FEFC) Sherriffs Orchard, Greyfriars Road, Coventry CV1 3PJ Tel: 020 353 0300 Responsible for the administration and funding related to all post-16 colleges.

Governors Associations
Action for Governors Information and Training (AGIT) c/o CEDC, Lyng Hall, Blackberry Lane, Coventry CV2 3JS Tel: 0203 638660
Institute of School and College Governors, 194 Freston Rd., London W10 6TT Tel: 081 968 8644 Also information and training for governors.
National Association of Governors and Managers (NAGM) Suite 36/38, 21 Bennetts Hill, Birmingham B2 5QP Tel: 021 643 5787 A membership organisation for governors.

Grant Maintained Schools Centre 36 Great Smith Street, London SW1 3BU Tel: 071 233 4666 Provides information about opting out.

Houses of Parliament
Switchboard for MP's and Peers Tel: 071 219 3000 When you get in touch ask for the direct line number for next time.
House of Commons, London SW1A 0AA Public Information Office Tel: 071 219 4272 Gives up to date information on Parliamentary matters including the stages which legislation has reached, membership of committees etc.
House of Lords, London SW1A 0AA Public Information Office Tel: 071 219 3107

Her Majesty's Stationery Office (HMSO) PO Box 276, London SW8 5DT Telephone orders 071 873 9090 Enquiries 071 873 0011 Publishes Hansard and other parliamentary papers including Select Committee reports and Statutory Instruments for which there is a charge.

Home and School Council 40 Sunningdale Mount, Ecclesall, Sheffield S11 9HA Tel: 0742 364181 Produces booklets for parents.

Human Scale Education Movement 96 Carlingcott, Nr. Bath BA2 8AW Tel: 0761 433733 Encourages learning communities structures along human scale lines.

Kidscape 152 Buckingham Palace Road, London SW1W 9TR Tel: 071 730 3300 Gives advice on dealing with bullying.

Kid's Clubs Network 279-281 Whitechapel Road, London E1 1BY Tel: 071 247 3009 Helps the setting up of after school clubs and playschemes.

Local Schools Information 1-5 Bath St., London EC1V 9QQ Tel: 071 490 4942 Fax: 071 250 1075 Provides information about opting out.

Office for Standards in Education (OFSTED) The Schools Inspectorate, Elizabeth House, York Road., London SE1 7PH

The National Centre for Able and Talented Children Park Campus, Boughton Green Road, Northampton NN2 7AL Tel: 0604 792300 Provides information about provision for very able children and local groups.

National Confederation of Parent Teacher Associations (NCPTA) 2 Ebbsfleet Industrial Estate, Stonebridge Rd., Gravesend, Kent DA11 9DZ Tel: 0474 560618 Will have contact addresses for local federations of PTA's.

National Curriculum Council (NCC) Albion Wharf, 25 Skeldergate, York YO1 2XL Tel: 0904 622533 Fax: 0904 622921 Provides information on the National Curriculum. Shortly to be amalgamated with SEAC.

National Association for Primary Education (NAPE) Queens Buildings, University of Leicester, Barracks Rd., Northampton NN2 6AF Tel: 0604 36326 Works on issues affecting primary school children, has local groups.

National Association for the Support of Small Schools The Cottage, Little Barningham, Norwich NR11 7LN Tel: 026 377 553 Campaigns to retain the village school.

Pre School Organisations

British Association for Early Childhood Education (BAECE) 111 City View House, 463 Bethnal Green Rd., London E2 9QH Tel: 071 739 7594

National Campaign for Nursery Education, 23 Albert Street, London NW1 7LU Tel: 071 387 6582

PreSchool Playgroups Association (PPA) 61-63 Kings Cross Rd., London WC1X 9LL Tel: 071 833 0991

Prime Minister 10 Downing Street, London SW1A 2AA

Religious Bodies Concerned with Education

Catholic Education Service, 41 Cromwell Road, London SW7 2DJ Tel: 071 584 7491

Free Church Federal Council, 27 Tavistock Square, London WC1H 9HH Tel: 071 387 8413

General Synod of the Church of England, Board of Education, Church House, Great Smith Street, London SW1P 3NZ Tel: 071 222 9011

School Meals Campaign P.O. BOX 402 WC1H 9TZ Tel: 071 383 7638 Campaigns for the reintroduction of nutritional guidelines for school meals.

Secretary of State for Education write to him/her at the Department for Education.

Special Education Needs (SEN) Organisations

ACE - see above.

Centre for the Studies of Integration in Education (CSIE), 415 Edgware Rd., London NW2 6NB Tel: 081 452 8642. Works towards the integration of all children with disabilities or learning difficulties in mainstream education.

Independent Panel for Special Education Advice, 12 Marsh Rd., Tillingham, Essex CM10 7SZ Tel: 0621 779781 Provides independent advice for parents.

National Association for Special Educational Needs, York House, Exhall Grange, Wheelwright Lane, Coventry CV7 9HP Tel: 0203 362414 Umbrella group for SEN organisations.

Network 81, 1-7 Woodfield Terrace, Chapel Hill, Stansted, Essex CM24 8AJ Tel: 0279 647415 A national network for parents.

Parents in Partnership, Top Portakabin, Clare House, St Georges Hospital, Blackshaw Rd., London SW17 0QT Tel: 081 767 3211 Support group for parents.

The Rathbone Society, 1st Floor, Princess House, 105-107 Princess St., Manchester M1 6DD Tel: 061 236 5358 Telephone help line for parents.

School Examination and Assessment Council (SEAC) Newcombe House, 45 Notting Hill Gate, London W11 3JB Tel: 071 229 1234 Fax: 071 229 8526 Produces information about the national system of assessment. Shortly to be amalgamated with the NCC.

Teaching Unions

Association of Teachers and Lecturers (ATL), 7 Northumberland St., London WC2N 5DA Tel: 071 930 6441

National Association of Headteachers (NAHT), 1 Heath Square, Boltro Rd., Haywards Heath, West Sussex RH16 1BL Tel: 0444 458133

National Assocation of Schoolmasters/Union of Women Teachers (NASUWT), Hillscourt Education Centre, Rednal, Birmingham B45 8RS Tel: 021 453 6150

National Association of Teachers in Further and Higher Education (NATFHE), 27 Britannia St., London WC1X 9JP Tel: 071 837 3636

National Union of Teachers (NUT), Hamilton House, Mabledon Place, London WC1H 9BD Tel: 071 388 6191

Secondary Heads Association (SHA), 130 Regent Rd., Leicester LE1 7PG Tel: 0533 471797

Professional Association of Teachers (PAT), 99 Friar Gate, Derby DE1 1EZ. Tel: 0332 372337

Dates

Dates of meetings of sub committees, Education Committee and Council. This should be available from the local authority offices. Make sure you are clear about which meetings will set the budget for the forthcoming year - so that you are not too late to influence decisions. Also find out about any local consultations and the dates on which they come to an end.

Date of next local elections - could make all the difference! - contact the local authority.

Surgeries of the local MP (from their constituency office in the phone book). Some local councillors have surgeries too - contact them directly.

End of consultation dates - of White Papers, Circulars etc from Government - contact the DFE.

Dates for consideration of Bills and meetings of committees in Parliament - contact Information Offices in both Houses.

Useful Publications

The following are useful and should be available in a good reference library.

Newspapers and Magazines

Education pages *Guardian* (Tuesday), *Times, Daily Telegraph* (Monday) *Independent* (Thursday)

Times Education Supplement (Friday)

Education, published by Longmans (weekly)

Reference Books

Hansard - proceedings of Parliament

The Law of Education, Butterworths

Longmans Education Yearbook, Longmans

Education Authorities Directory, School Government Publishing Company

British Education Index, Leeds University (only in specialist education libraries)

Editors from Media Directories, 9-10 Great Sutton Street, London EC1V 0BX. Lists national and local media, addresses, phone and fax.

Dod's Parliamentary Companion, Hurst Green, East Sussex TN19 7PX (Biographical details of Peers and MP's).

Vacher's Parliamentary Companion and *Vacher's Biographical Companion*, 113 High Street, Berkhamsted Herts HP4 2DJ (Details of Peers, MPs and senior civil servants.)

Books worth reading

Education A to Z; *Parents Information Checklist*; *Special Education Handbook*; *School Choice and Appeals* - from ACE (see above)

How to Run a Local Campaign, Polly Bird, Northcote House 1989

Lobbying. An Insider's Guide to the Parliamentary Process, Alf Dubbs, Pluto Press 1988

MEMBERSHIP

Members are entitled to one copy of the **CASE** magazine, *Parents and Schools*, six times a year; voting rights and representation on the National Executive Committee (NEC).

MEMBERSHIP FORM

Please make cheques payable to **CASE** and send to **CASE** 158 Durham Road, London, SW20 0DG *(Note: Paying by Bankers Order helps cut down administration costs so your membership fee goes even further.)*

Name . . . .

Address . . . .

. . . .

Postcode . . . . Telephone . . . .

I enclose
My membership fee of £10 (£5 unwaged) £
My donation £ ______________
Total £ ______________

You may be contacted by other **CASE** members in your area for local campaigns. If you do **NOT** wish to be contacted please tick the box. ☐

If there is a local group in your area you will find a contact number in *Parents and Schools*. If you want to start a local group, tick the box for a free leaflet. ☐

BANKERS ORDER

[NB Please send this form to **CASE**, NOT to the Bank]

To the Manager . . . . Bank

Branch address . . . .

Please pay £. . . . . from my a/c no. . . . . sort code . . . .
to the CASE a/c no. 80237426 sort code 20-91-94 held at Barclay's Bank, Watlington OX9 5PY commencing on. . . . . and annually on that date thereafter until otherwise notified.

Name . . . .

Address . . . .

Postcode . . . . Signed . . . .

For office use only: **BANK please quote reference number** . . . .